IMAGES OF ENGLAND

URMSTON, FLIXTON AND DAVYHULME

Woods Farm and Wesleyan Chapel, Moorside Road, Davyhulme.

IMAGES OF ENGLAND

URMSTON, FLIXTON AND DAVYHULME

KAREN CLIFF AND VICKI MASTERSON

TEMPUS

Petrol pumps on Lostock Road, Davyhulme in the 1920s.

First published 2000, reprinted 2002, 2006

Tempus Publishing Limited
The Mill, Brimscombe Port,
Stroud, Gloucestershire, GL5 2QG

© Karen Cliff and Vicky Masterson, 2002

British Library Cataloguing in Publication Data.
A catalogue record for this book is available from the British Library.

ISBN 0 7524 2162 X

Typesetting and origination by Tempus Publishing Limited
Printed in Great Britain

Contents

Carrington Road, Flixton, c. 1900.

Bibliography

Hoare, E.M. (1998) *Trafford General Hospital (Park): A History*
Langton, D.H. (1898) *History of the Parish of Flixton Comprising the Townships of Flixton and Urmston*
Lawson, R. (1898) *A History of Flixton Urmston and Davyhulme*
Lee, D.W. (1976) *The Flixton Footpath Battle*
Leech, Sir Bosdin. (1907) *History of the Manchester Ship Canal from its Inception to its Completion*, 2 vols
Nevill, M. (1997) *The Archaeology of Trafford*
Owen, D. (1977) *Canals to Manchester*
Rendell, D. (1998) *Cinemas of Trafford*
Spencer, Revd A. (1898) *A History of Methodism in Davyhulme*
University of Manchester Archaeological Unit (1996) *Bromyhurst Farm Barn: a Study of an Eighteenth-Century Type 1 Threshing Barn*

Introduction

Urmston, Flixton and Davyhulme now form part of the Metropolitan Borough of Trafford. Situated on the northern side of the river Mersey, they were once in the county of Lancashire, and from 1849 until the end of the nineteenth century, the townships were included in the Barton-upon-Irwell Union. In 1894 the Local Government Act was passed, and the county council converted Urmston into an urban district, while Flixton and Davyhulme remained under the rural district of Barton-upon-Irwell. The area has experienced several changes of local government since these early years. In 1933, Urmston Urban District absorbed Flixton and Davyhulme, and in 1974 Trafford Metropolitan Borough in turn absorbed the three townships.

The history of the area is largely a story of increasing population and housing developments. Flixton was at one time more populated and considered more important than Urmston, which until the late nineteenth century was a predominantly rural area. There are no stirring national historical events to speak of, for instance Urmston was one of the few places where Mary Queen of Scots was *not* imprisoned, and as far as we know it did not feature as one of the places where Cromwell and Charles I slept overnight on their way to and from battles! The history of the Urmston area is no less interesting for this lack of royal attention, since its growth resulted from two of the most innovative and daring schemes in the world, namely the Bridgewater Canal, established in the eighteenth century, and the Manchester Ship Canal which had revolutionised the whole of the north-west, if not the whole of Britain, by the end of the nineteenth century. Though the urban and industrial heritage may not appeal so much as the romantic version of history, it is perhaps more important to know how the area was shaped and how this industrial development affected peoples' daily lives. In this book Karen Cliff and Vicki Masterson show Urmston, Flixton and Davyhulme at the grass roots level, and the photographs from the collection housed at Trafford Local Studies Centre reveal life as it has been for the last one hundred years.

Pat Southern
Trafford Local Studies Librarian
2000

Acknowledgments

All the photographs in this book are held at Trafford Local Studies Centre. The authors would like to thank Mr H. Cuthbert of Urmston for permission to reproduce photographs from the Cuthbert collection, housed at the Local Studies Centre.

A Sunday School procession on Crofts Bank Road, Urmston, Whit Sunday, 1913.

One

Farming and Industry

Today, it is hard to imagine that the Urmston area was once a rural community with many of the inhabitants living and working on the land. Although there was some industry, the farms themselves supplied work for many people. The land provided good soil for wheat but most farms were worked mainly at subsistence level with little being produced for open sale. Most of the farms have now gone but a few still remain to remind us of our rural past, such as Shawe Hey Farm on Church Road, Flixton.

In 1841 the land was owned by fifty-one people with only two people holding over one hundred acres. The average size of a farm was around thirty acres and consisted of meadow, pasture and arable with few cattle. Many of the farmers also owned cottages, which they rented to the handloom weavers.

Prior to the demolition of Hillam Farm in Urmston and Bromyhurst Farm in Davyhulme, an archaeological survey was carried out at each site. The information obtained has provided us with a valuable insight on the history and development of farming in the Urmston area, which we would otherwise have lost.

Although the main occupation in the area was farming, spinning and weaving also played an important role. Flixton had two mills, Calamanco Mill that stood by the side of the river Irwell between Hulmes Bridge ferry and Irlam ferry, and Stotts Mill on Flixton Road, Flixton. Stotts Mill, owned by James and Adam Stott, opened in 1851 and employed over four hundred men and women. The mill was steam-powered with water supplied from a 300ft deep well and four reservoirs. The reservoirs were located in the Bowfell Road area of Flixton. In 1879 the mill was almost destroyed by fire but continued to function until the 1930s when it finally closed. A drill hall was built on the site, which is used today as private school.

The *Western Telegraph* newspaper was first produced in 1895 from premises on Woodsend Road, Flixton. When the newspaper moved to a new office in Urmston, the site was taken over by the Pybus Candle Works, which continued to trade until 1974.

By the early 1960s Urmston Town centre had changed very little with local shops running along the side of Station Road, Flixton Road and Crofts Bank Road. The small shops had catered for every need in the past but the local council decided the area needed modernizing in order to compete with other towns. Plans were put into place for a new development, which included a supermarket. Winifred Road was demolished to make way for the new shopping centre and in 1970 the first premises on Moorfield Walk were opened.

With the building of the railway in 1873 and the growth in population, pressure was placed on the farmers and landowners to release land for housing. The landowners in the Flixton area were more reluctant to sell which led to the Urmston area developing at a much faster rate than Flixton. The gradual change from a rural to a modern community can be attributed both to the building of the railway and also the effects of the Industrial Revolution on the area.

Croft Hall Farm, Davyhulme, 1907. This farm was situated on Barton Road.

The barn at Bethells Farm, Lostock Road, Davyhulme in the 1920s.

Lostock Farm, Davyhulme in the 1920s.

Bromyhurst Farm, Davyhulme, 1977. The Harrison family built the farm during the eighteenth century; a date stone bears the date of 1705. The farm was a threshing barn with a shippon for five cows. The 174 acres were once part of the large estates belonging to the De Trafford family but passed into the hands of the Manchester Ship Canal Company. The area was once part of the Barton conservation area. The farm was demolished during the late 1990s to make way for the Trafford Centre.

Farmyard and carts at Fold Farm, Davyhulme Road, Davyhulme.

Rudyards Farm, Davyhulme. The farm was situated behind the Nags Head public house; it supplied milk for sale.

Davyhulme Hall Farm, 1927. The farm faced Moorside Road and for centuries had been in the possession of Davyhulme Hall.

Davyhulme Hall Farm, Davyhulme. The farm was situated close to Moorside Road, and was demolished in 1927. The photograph features the barn and beyond the teamsmen's cottages.

Sticken's Farm, Davyhulme, thought to have been built in 1723.

Sticken's Farm, Bent Lanes, Davyhulme. The farm was sold at auction by Edwin Bradshaw & Son Ltd on Monday 17 January 1938. The lot included two tons of pigs' potatoes and a quantity of swedes.

Lime Tree Farm, Urmston, 1936. The farm stood where Churchgate is today.

Newcroft Farm, Urmston.

Acregate Farm, Flixton. The farmhouse was originally built in 1869 and included two barns and sixty acres of land. The fields extended to the banks of the River Mersey and the river often flooded the lower lying land. When the Manchester Ship Canal opened in 1894, it provided a channel for drainage and the problem improved. Dairy cattle were the main feature of this farm. The photograph shows cattle being fed during a cold winter in 1963. The farm was nearly destroyed in 1972 when the barn caught fire and seventy tons of hay were destroyed.

De Brook Farm, Flixton. The farm was situated on land close to De Brook Court in Flixton and included the land where Wellacre Secondary School stands today. At one time it produced barley, oats, potatoes and root vegetables. During the 1960s the farm fell into decline and was eventually demolished.

16

Whiteheads Farm, Flixton, 1903. The farm was situated where Brooklyn Avenue is today. The photograph shows labourers haymaking.

Hillam Farm, Urmston, 1970. The earliest references to Hillam Farm go back to the sixteenth century; Trafford MBC holds a document dated 1609. The ownership of the farm passed through four families with a succession of tenants including Urmston District Council in 1957. The farm was the subject of an archaeological survey prior to its demolition in 1986.

Hillam Farm, Urmston. The photograph was taken in 1985, just prior to demolition.

Auburn Lodge Farm, Urmston, 1979.

Warburton Wall Farm, Flixton, 1930. The farm was situated on Irlam Road close to the ferry terminus.

Towngate Farm, Flixton. The farm was on the opposite side of Irlam Road to Warburton Wall Farm.

Shaw Hey Farm, Flixton. This farm is one of the few that remain in the area. The fifty-two acre farm is sited on low-lying ground close to the River Mersey and has been flooded many times in its history. In 1966 it was almost destroyed when the barn caught fire, killing fifty pigs as a result.

Shaw Hey Farm, Flixton in flood, 1946.

Brook Farm, Flixton, 1890. The farm was situated on Western Road, Flixton.

Willows Farm, Flixton, looking from Chassen Road.

Pybus Candle Works, Flixton, 1973. The Pybus Candle factory was at one time the second largest manufacturer of candles in the country. The Pybus brothers started the Flixton factory in Woodsend Road in 1937. The company was later sold to a polish company in 1973.

Simpson Ready Foods, Urmston, 1973. William and Gertrude Simpson started the firm in 1911. It produced ready-made tinned foods for both home and export. The factory is still in production today.

Coupe Brickwork's situated in Flixton. The land area provided a good clay soil for the making of bricks.

Hoes Sauce Factory. The factory was situated on Urmston Lane and produced bottled sauces. Trafford Local Studies Centre holds one of the original bottles used by the company.

Stotts Mill, Flixton. James and Adam Stott built the mill in 1851; it was situated on Flixton Road close to the Bird in Hand public house. The mill carried bleaching, dyeing weaving and finishing and produced fabric for the clothing industry. The mill employed a large number of people and provided work for many out of work hand-loom weavers as their industry declined. The row of terraced cottages, which stood opposite the mill on Flixton Road, was built for the mill workers. When the mill was demolished in 1936 the rubble obtained was used to fill in the mill reservoirs, which were sited where Bowfell road is today. In 1939 the houses had to give up their gardens for the road to be widened.

Cuthbert's Butcher, Urmston 1913. The shop was situated on Crofts Bank Road and is one of the few family businesses which continue to this day. The photograph shows a delivery boy with his bike outside the shop. The shop next door was a jeweller's shop which was owned by Thomas Titley.

Blomley's Butcher, Urmston in the 1900s. Fresh meat was often seen hung outside the shop. The delivery horse and trap is in the front of the picture.

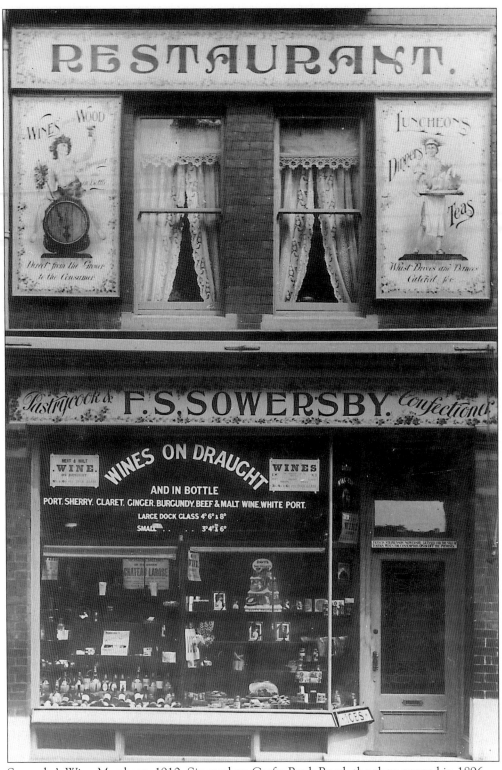

Sowersby's Wine Merchant, 1910. Situated on Crofts Bank Road, the shop opened in 1896.

The creamery, Urmston, 1913. The creamery produced its own butter and cream and provided a milk delivery service. The shop was situated on Crofts Bank Road where Silcock's greengrocer is today.

Cattle on Stretford Road, 1913. The cattle seen here have just been purchased at the market and are on their way to Cuthbert's Butcher shop in Urmston where they would be slaughtered.

Crofts Bank Road, Urmston. William Deacons bank was situated on the corner of Crofts Bank Road and Railway Road, where the Royal Bank of Scotland is today.

Collector of Bones and Fat, 1913. The bone merchant seen here on Flixton Road is a sight not seen anymore. The advertisements in the background show products which are still available today.

Two

Transport, Roads and Footpaths

Urmston and Flixton were once isolated settlements, bordered on one side by the River Mersey and on the other by the River Irwell. Mainly agricultural, the land was traversed by many footpaths and byways with few main roads. Many of the old footpaths are now public rights of way and the most famous – the Bottoms Footpath – has recently been awarded a Blue Plaque to commemorate the celebrated victory of 1827 when the people of Flixton won the right to use it after Squire Wright had it closed.

There were no bridges to cross the Mersey and Irwell rivers, nor were there any great roads to connect to surrounding districts. The roads that did exist led mainly to the three fords by which these rivers were crossed and along which passed, after 1750, packet boats carrying passengers, and flat boats carrying goods. Many of these fords later became ferries, and eventually various bridges were built, including Hulme Bridge and Carrington Bridge. When the Manchester Ship Canal was opened in 1894 by Queen Victoria, the ferries were funded by the Manchester Ship Canal Company and the packet boats ceased. The canal provided the first access to the sea for Manchester.

Before 1845 villagers had to walk to Stretford to catch either the stagecoach or the two-horse omnibus that left the Angel Hotel every hour for Manchester. In 1873 railway stations were opened in Flixton and Urmston and the horse bus was discontinued. Local people were opposed to the railway, and in Flixton landowners tried to discourage building by not selling their land. The advent of the railway changed the nature of the area considerably and it became a prime location for residence. More land was bought up for housing, and in turn there was a demand for a better road system.

The 1846 Ordnance Survey map shows the principal roads for the Urmston, Flixton, and Davyhulme area as: Shaw Lane/Church Lane, Green Lane/Millers Lane, Smithy Lane/Cockedge Lane, Flash Lane/Moorside, Woodsend Lane, Davyhulme Lane, Urmston Lane and Gammershaw Lane. While many of the old road names seem unfamiliar to us today, some have survived with only slight modification. Church Road, as we know it today was originally known as Shaw Lane and Church Lane. Gammershaw Lane has since been renamed Stretford Road whilst Cockedge Lane has now become Flixton Road.

Road transport moved straight from horse and trap or the horse buses, to motorised buses, the first of which was the Blue Motor Bus Service Limited in 1923. This was later sold to the Northwest Road Car Company Limited.

The most important road development was the opening of the M63 in 1960. It was hoped that it would solve the problems encountered by traffic particularly at Barton Bridge, which is narrow and can cause traffic build up when it swings open. The construction of the motorway bridge over the Ship Canal cost the life of one worker. Unfortunately, the motorway at this point was still inadequate and had to be extended in 1984.

Moorside Road, Flixton, *c.* 1900. Moorside Road was originally called Flash Lane, or 'The Flash', at the Flixton end, and 'Moorside' leading into Urmston. The white cottage, which can be seen on the left was the old poorhouse, and was situated close to Flixton Cricket Club.

Flixton Road, Flixton, 1939. The village Smith was situated on the corner of Irlam and Flixton Road at the point where the bus stop is today. It was demolished in the early 1950s.

Church Road, Flixton, in the 1930s. This area of Flixton was originally known as Shaw Town and was often called School Green, as the first schools in the parish were built there. The Roebuck public house can be seen on the left with its original entrance, which was on Chassen Road. The white building on the right was once the parish Tithe Barn, one of two for Flixton. It was used to store the tithes for St Michael's church. A tithe was the tenth part of a farmer's produce, paid to the church annually as a form of rent. The barn was later used as a garage until it was demolished in the 1990s to make way for new housing. Chassen Road, which can be seen at the junction, was once known as Penny Lane, the name derived from the fact that travellers had to pay a penny toll to pass along it. A link with the past still survives as the bridge over the railway, called Penny Bridge, still bears the name.

Western Road, Flixton. The footpath followed the route of Western Road. This photograph was taken looking towards Irlam Road. The rural setting gives some indication of how the area once looked.

Flixton Road, Flixton in the 1930s. Flixton was once a thriving shopping area. The photograph shows the post office, William Deacons Bank, Browns grocers, Johnson's greengrocers, and Johnson's bakery, and at the end of the terrace, Martin's Bank. Opposite this stood Millatt's barn, which housed the Boot and Shoe repairers and Gibbins' pork butchers.

Ambleside Road, Flixton, c. 1930. The photograph shows the road before it was completed. The houses have been recently built; you can see the fence running along the bottom of the picture where the road finishes. As more of the surrounding land became available, the road was lengthened and more houses were built.

Davyhulme Road, Davyhulme, 1906. Looking towards Davyhulme Circle, St Mary's church can be seen on the right. Slater's Directory for 1898 describes Davyhulme as a hamlet one and a half miles south-west of Barton, with two churches, a sewage works, one school and a post office. The postmistress was Mrs Sarah Bethel.

Bent Lanes, Davyhulme, with a pony and trap close to the path leading to Stickens farm.

Calderbank, Davyhulme, *c.* 1920.

Higher Road, Urmston. The Primitive Methodist Chapel is on the right. It was built in 1873, due to the efforts of William Johnson, a local Methodist. The Trafford Arms can be seen on the left.

Chadwick Lane, Urmston, 1954. Now called Bradfield Road, this road was still cobbled in 1954.

Pony and trap on Princess Road, Urmston, in the 1900s.

Lime Avenue, Urmston, 1931.

Looking down Albert Avenue from Higher Road, 1932. The gates to the Jewish Cemetery can be seen at the bottom. In the late nineteenth century, thousands of Jewish people settled in Britain and many made their homes in the north. The cemetery is one of the main Jewish burial grounds in the area, with over two thousand people being buried here. There is another entrance in Chapel Grove.

Crofts Bank Road, Urmston, 1913, looking towards Davyhulme Circle. The building on the right is now used as a doctor's surgery. The creamery, which can just be seen on the left, was situated where Silcock's greengrocery is today.

Flixton Road, Urmston, 1913. The Co-operative Society on the left was opened in 1901, and was described as a, 'grocery, drapery, boot and shoe, butchering, milk and reading room'. It was located close to the entrance of Moorfield Walk. The Eccles Provident Industrial Co-operative Society provided a range of services including a library, which supplied the latest books, newspapers and periodicals. The children in the photograph are taking part in a Sunday School procession, which was a regular feature of the church calendar.

Station Bridge, Urmston, 1912. The public house on the right of the photograph was the Victoria Hotel; it was the terminus for the horse buses which ran between Urmston and Stretford. Railway Road seen on the left was often used by cab drivers to tether their horses while waiting for a fare.

Station Road, Urmston in the 1900s. The large building on the left is the Liberal Club, which was built in 1891; it was originally called the Gladstone Building after W.E. Gladstone. The milk cart can be seen on the right.

Crofts Bank Road, Urmston. This part of Crofts Bank Road is now Davyhulme Circle. The large building is the Nag's Head public house, with the horse bus just visible outside. The knife grinder can be seen pushing his cart towards Urmston.

Moorside Road, Urmston, 1913. The lady in the centre of the photo is Mrs Ellen Cuthbert, shown with her family. They are standing at the side of Carrs Ditch, believed to be an ancient Roman fortification which passed through Flixton and Urmston. The ditch formed the boundary between Urmston and Davyhulme. Excavation of the ditch has revealed that it was a minor fortification about fifteen feet wide with a bank about twelve feet rising from the ditch bottom.

Church Road, Urmston, 1912, looking towards Flixton. A horse and carriage is just visible.

Crofts Bank Road, Urmston, 1928. Cuthbert's butchers shop is on the left.

Carrington Bridge, 1907. In the 1600s a wooden bridge was built across the River Mersey by Lady Carrington so that people from Carrington could attend St Michael's church. The wooden bridge was only a footbridge, so any vehicle that wanted to cross had to pass over the ford. This was then replaced in 1840 by an iron bridge..

The River Mersey, before 1909. Flixton church is in the background.

Barton Bridge, before 1898. This bridge was built in 1681 and is said to have been demolished to stop Bonnie Prince Charlie passing over it on his way south. St Catherine's church is in the background.

Barton Bridge, c. 1960. This bridge was built when the Manchester Ship Canal was constructed to replace the three arch stone bridge which was built in 1876 by Brindley, thus allowing tall-masted ships to travel up and down the canal. The bridge weighs 800 tons, is 195ft long, 25ft wide and is turned on sixty-four steel rollers powered by a hydraulic mechanism.

Barton Bridge, c. 1970. It was not unusual for the bridge to become stuck on hot days and the fire brigade would come and pour cold water on it to reduce the temperature.

Barton Aqueduct, Manchester Ship Canal

Valentine's Series

Barton Aqueduct with a barge crossing the aqueduct from the Eccles side.

Barton Aqueduct, 1962. The Bridgewater Canal was taken across the Manchester Ship Canal by this aqueduct, built by Leader Williams. It was a great engineering achievement of its

time. The moveable section was very heavy and the ends had to be made watertight when the bridge was swung.

A ship passing through Barton Bridge on the Manchester Ship Canal, 1913.

The horse bus, Stretford Road, Urmston, 1907. The bus which went down Flixton Road, Irlam Road, Woodsend Road, Calderbank, Davyhulme Road to the Nags Head, then on to Urmston and Stretford, began its life as the horse and cab of Mr Bate of Reade House who used it for his own private purposes. Other gentlemen shared the cab and it eventually became the forerunner of the bus service.

Horse Omnibus outside the Victoria Hotel, Urmston, 1913. The bus ran to the Old Cock Hotel, Stretford.

The horse bus on Urmston Lane.

Irlam ferry, 1935. This ferry was crossed by a bridge made by the builders of the Manchester Ship Canal. When the canal was finished a boat for passengers was provided together with one for horses.

Hulmes Bridge, 1890. This was located behind the Fox and Hounds pub and was replaced by the free ferry.

Urmston station, 1913. Urmston and Flixton stations opened 2 September 1873. The Duke of York public house was demolished to accommodate Urmston station. The contractors (ticket holders) from both Urmston and Flixton numbered twelve but by 1898, Urmston station had issued 1,225 contracts whereas Flixton numbered only 235. Both stations however, were busy with goods yards for coal.

Pony and trap outside Flixton station, 1900. The man at the reins is Jack Royal. Mr Barnaby, the stationmaster at Flixton in 1898, won the first prize for the best garden in the line for twelve years. The 1898 Ordnance Survey map of Flixton shows these gardens which include a fountain.

Pony and trap. The photograph was taken outside Cuthbert's shop on Crofts Bank Road, and

shows the Cuthbert family ready for an outing in 1913

Tetlow's bus at the pumps, 1927. In 1908, two brothers, Harry and James Tetlow came to live in Urmston and started the Blue Bus Service in 1923. The routes ran from Flixton Road, Woodsend Road, and Irlam Road to Flixton and Urmston stations. There was also a service from the Nag's Head to Stretford via Lostock Road and Derbyshire Lane.

Northwestern bus, 1928. Mid Cheshire Motor Company had a depot for five buses on Chassen Road. North Western Bus Company acquired these premises in 1924. They then bought Tetlow and Collier in 1928, and H. & J. Tetlow in 1938. The Higher Road bus station opened in 1824.

Manchester Ship Canal, with *H.M.S. Orpheus* passing through Flixton. This was possibly the last time a submarine made the passage to the port of Manchester.

Dr Mayne's trap, *c*. 1900. This is the entrance to Flash Farm on Woodsend Road looking towards the Union Inn.

Donkey and cart outside The Lindens, Lostock Road. Robert Estill with Ruth, Belby and

George Estill in the trap.

A boy on a bike on Ciss Lane.

Winifred Road, Urmston in the 1940s. By the August of 1965 the houses on Winifred Road had been flattened and the residents re-housed. Work began soon after on the foundations for the new shopping centre.

Stretford Road, Urmston 1962, looking towards Stretford. The telephone box marks the boundary between Urmston and Stretford. On the Urmston side, the road is named Stretford Road but on the Stretford side it changes to Urmston Lane.

Stretford Road, Urmston, 1962. looking from Stretford towards the junction with Church Road. Note how quiet the road is. The traffic lights have not been installed yet and looking at the picture you can see why – not a car in sight.

Dumplington Lane, 1910, looking towards Davyhulme Circle. Dumplington Lane was renamed Redcliffe Road but changed again during the late 1990s to Trafford Boulevard when the Trafford Centre opened. It seems ironic that with the amount of traffic which passes along the road today, in 1906 Davyhulme Parish Council refused the Trafford Park Estate Company permission to run their omnibuses along it as they said, 'It was dangerous for mechanically propelled vehicles to run along this stretch of roadway'.

Dumplington Circle, 1951. Prior to the building of the motorway the only way to approach Eccles from Davyhulme was to cross the Manchester Ship Canal over Barton Swing Bridge via Dumplington Circle.

Moorside Road, Flixton, 1958. These cottages, Nos 141-149, stood on Moorside Road at the junction with Malvern Avenue. The black and white building, which is just visible, is Wesley Cottage.

Alderley Road, Flixton, 1906.

Flixton village, 1959, before Church Road was widened. The shop and houses on the right face the Greyhound Public House. The village is one of the oldest areas of Flixton; two cottages, which still survive today, date back to 1672.

Marlborough Road, Flixton. The Bowker family had their family residence on the corner of Moorside Road where the corner of Marlborough Road is today. The surrounding fields were known as Bowker's fields.

Railway Road, Urmston, looking towards Stretford with the railway on the right, in the 1890s. The Royle Higginson family started Urmston market, which is situated on Railway Road. It is one of the few private markets in the country.

Lostock Road with the view towards Davyhulme. Bennett's farm is situated on the right.

Whitelake Avenue, Flixton, 1920. The tithe map for Flixton, dated 1843, shows that the fields around this area of Flixton were known as White leach.

Moss Vale Road, 1958. The houses and shop were demolished in 1958 to make way for the motorway.

Grosvenor Road, Urmston, 1905. The road was originally known as Lily Street.

Western Road, Flixton, started out as an ancient by-way, later developing into a cart road until it finally became residential in 1892 and was known as Bruce Road. The local authority decided to rename it; names favoured were Moffat Road, Livingstone Road or Western Road. Dr Moffat was a former missionary, living in a cottage on Bruce Road who had been responsible for translating the bible into an African language, and his daughter had married the famous missionary Dr Livingstone. The names were put to ballot with the majority in favour of Western Road.

Irlam Road, Flixton, 1906. Irlam Road was once known as Miller's Lane up to the Red Lion, then Boat Lane to the edge of the Manchester Ship Canal. The distance across the canal at this point is 370ft and at one time a ferry ran between Flixton and Irlam.

Three

Leisure

Leisure pastimes have changed a great deal through the ages although there are many links with the past that still survive. Most entertainment was centred on the church year and the word holiday itself is derived from the word holy day.

The Flixton Wakes were celebrated on the first Sunday after 11 October each year, and involved games, sack races, fighting and foot races. Booths were erected around the area close to St Michael's church and people would come from miles around to see the amusements. The wakes continue to this day in the form of the annual carnival.

Many sports involved bloodletting, both to animals and humans. The Nelson, Roebuck and Red Lion Pubs were all famous for badger, bull and bear baiting with bets being taken on the outcome. However, it was the alehouse keepers themselves who decided that the sport was too cruel and applied to the local justices to have it stopped, even though they stood to lose the most from lost income!

As the old pastimes died out new ones replaced them: Social Clubs, Temperance Societies, and Literary Societies were founded. The Urmston Cricket and Lawn Tennis Club was opened in 1846, the Lacrosse Club in 1885 and the Rifle Club in 1899. People also began to read more for leisure with public libraries becoming more popular. Many of the local pubs provided picnic areas for families. Flixton also had a public baths, which was situated on Flixton Road.

During the 1920s and 1930s Urmston Council pursued a policy of acquiring lands as they became available, in order to safeguard local amenities and also to provide new ones. Davvyhulme Park and Golden Hill Park were built during the 1920s and first appear on the Ordance Survey map around 1928. Davyhulme Park had a large paddling pool, a floral garden and two small ponds where children could use fishing nets to fish for small fish. A visit to the local park was a regular day out for many families who would bring a picnic and spend the whole day there.

In 1935 Urmston Coucil bought the Worthington-Wright Estate in Flixton, which included Flixton House and 218 acres of land. The land was originally farmland and included Acre Gare Farm. After the farm closed down, the land was used to provide the William Wroe municipal golf course and Flixton House was made available for public use. In Davyhulme, Mr A.T. Lees bequeathed 9 acres of land to the council for 'Public Pleasure or Rest Gardens' which is still known today as Lees Playing Fields.

During the early 1920s cinema became a new source of entertainment. The Urmston Picture Palace was opened in 1913, the Empress in 1929 and the Curzon in 1931.

Red Lion Hotel, Flixton. Originally called the Lion, the pub attracted large numbers of people who visited the area especially during the Whitsun holidays to picnic on the green. It was demolished in 1967.

Flixton Road, Flixton. The Bird in Hand public house can be seen behind the white cottages. The brick building in the far right of the photograph was the site of the first public baths in Flixton. They were built by Messrs Stott of Stotts Mill and consisted of slipper baths with one large plunge bath. The baths were demolished in the early 1900s.

Greyhound Hotel, Flixton, originally licensed in 1788.

Church Inn, Flixton. The photograph shows the Church Inn as it used to look.

Nags Head public house, Davyhulme, 1907. In 1899 the *Western Telegraph* newspaper ran an advertisement which read, 'Picnics, Wedding and other parties receive every attention. Billiards, Excellent Bowling Green and Good Stabling. Mrs R. Cronshaw, Proprietress'. The lamp-post, used here as a signpost, informs us that Urmston is three quarters of a mile away and Barton Bridge one and a quarter miles from this point.

The old Nags Head public house, Davyhulme, 1870. The publican was John Chapman.

Lord Nelson public house, Urmston, 1888. Situated on Stretford Road it was built in 1805 and named after Admiral Nelson. It was originally built in plain brick but over the years alterations have changed its appearance. The pub stands on the site of the old Court Baron, a place where the Lord of the Manor would sit in judgement. The pub was still used as a courthouse until as late as 1890.

Moorside Road, Flixton. The children are from the Methodist Sunday School and are seen here dancing around the Maypole. The field was situated where Trevor Road and Mardale Avenue are now.

Paddling Pool, Davyhulme Park in the 1940s. Parks were a favourite place for entertainment and were well cared for.

Golden Hill Park in the 1920s, with the opening of the August Bank holiday flower show.

Golden Hill Park, 1903.

Urmston Baths in the 1970s.

Urmston Baths undergoing construction in 1932. They were opened to the public in 1933 at a cost of £31,000. The glazed dome rose to a height of fifty feet. The pool was 100ft in length and had a capacity of 180,000 gallons. A special feature was the fitting of a wooden floor over the pool, which enabled dancing and public meetings to be held there. The baths were closed in the 1980s.

Coronation Arch, Urmston, 1902. The Coronation Arch was built to celebrate the coronation of Edward VII in 1902. The arch was sited over Station Bridge in Urmston and was built by Joseph Spark, joiners and builders, who held premises in Urmston. The whole of Urmston was decorated with flags to celebrate the occasion.

Coronation Day, Urmston, 1902. Station Road looking towards the station.

Urmston Carnival in the 1920s. The Urmston and District Carnival held each year, has a long history and the event itself has changed little through the years. It would begin with a parade, and culminate in the crowning of the Rose Queen. In 1935 the Rose Queen was a lady named Patricia Whitehead and her dress cost the princely sum of £3 5s. The carnival and later the Urmston show provided entertainment for all the local people which included vegetable displays, horse riding, music and dancing competitions and would continue into the evening. In 1963 the organizers managed to persuade an up and coming northern band called The Beatles to perform at the show. It was a unique event, which many people will remember, but unfortunately was never repeated.

Urmston Carnival, held in Chassen Park in the 1920s, showing the fancy dress competition.

Boys dressed as soldiers at Urmston Carnival in the 1920s.

Allotment Society, 1932; Urmston was renowned for its allotments, which were largely under the control of the Urmston and District Allotment Society. A large horticultural show was held annually where members could meet socially and show off their produce. The Granville Park Group, seen in this picture, appear to have won a prize.

A garden party held in the Mossfield Allotments on Flixton road, 1913.

Empress Cinema, Urmston, 1962. Urmston once had three cinemas – the Empress, the Urmston Picture Palace and the Curzon. The only one that survives today is the Curzon. The Empress Cinema opened in 1929 and held 900 people. The film advertised in the picture was called *Secret Partner*. The cinema closed in 1958 and was demolished in 1962.

The Library, Flixton.

Flixton library in the 1950s. Flixton library opened in 1939 at a cost of £6,831. The library was a very popular place for both children and adults.

Children's Book Week at Flixton Library, 1949.

Davyhulme Park, showing the formal gardens and archway.

The Carnival, 1975, with the Flixton Krickettes seen here on Station Road, Urmston.

Flixton Silver Band, 1968. The band was formed in 1967, and under the direction of Paul Crashly entertained people from the Urmston area for many years, playing at local events. Flixton was also famous for two earlier bands, the Flixton Village Band, formed in 1889 and the Flixton Prize Band which played during the 1930s. The Flixton Village band played at Irlam in 1894 when Queen Victoria opened the Manchester Ship Canal.

Flixton Carnival, 1919, held in the grounds of Flixton Cricket Club; the Bonny Baby contest was a popular event.

Garrick's Head, Flixton in the 1930s. The old Garrick's Head was demolished around 1928. A plan and line drawing of the pub suggests that at one time it was a thatched cottage. The taproom used daily by customers consisted of a stone floor furnished with fixed settles around two large tables.

Four

Halls and Houses

Urmston, Flixton and Davyhulme have changed dramatically over the 150 years. At the beginning of the twentieth century it was largely a rural community. Between 1801 and 1851, the occupation shown on the census was predominantly agricultural and the housing reflected this, consisting of farmhouses, labourer's cottages and the much larger Halls or houses of the wealthy landowners. There were a number of ancient families residing in the area, including the Warburtons, who for a time lived in Newcroft Hall; the de Traffords, a branch of whom lived in Urmston Hall, and the Hulmes of Davyhulme.

Urmston Hall lay to the south of Urmston around five miles from Manchester. It was situated near the banks of the River Mersey. Adam de Ormeston held the manor of Urmston follows by his son Richard. Adam's daughter married Ralph Hyde and the Hall was mentioned by William Hyde in 1587, his ancestors living there until the twentieth century. It then passed through marriage to the Hulme family. From the mid-1800s the Hall was used as a farm by the Stott family, and was then demolished in 1937. Newcroft Hall lay between Stretford and Urmston. In its day it was the oldest Hall in the immediate area, and was surrounded by a moat. Richard Warburton lived there in 1397 and later it was the home of the Radcliffe family. Richard Radcliffe was buried in the porch of Flixton church in 1602. Davyhulme Hall was the seat of John de Hulme in the reign of Henry II (1154-1189) and the family continued there for many generations. The hall and grounds were sold in 1735 to William Allen, a banker who became bankrupt in 1789. Then followed Robert Norris who left it to his nephew Mr Entwistle. Davyhulme Hall was demolished in 1888.

Shawe Hall was originally surrounded by a moat and was rebuilt by Lawerence Asshawe in the 1600s. After various owners and being used at one time as a Ladies School, it was bought by Col. Ridehalgh whose family resided there until the Second World War.

The building and subsequent opening of the Manchester Ship Canal, which linked Manchester with a seaport, and the later the sale of Trafford Park, the seat of the de Trafford family for many generations, led to the development of the surrounding area. By the 1901 census, agricultural work had ceased to be a category of occupation and the population of the Trafford area more than trebled.

- As Trafford Park grew into the largest industrial estate in Europe, the need for housing grew. In 1851 the census recorded 142 dwellings in Urmston compared to 1445 in 1901. We see much of the farmland being built upon as we reach the era of the modern semi-detached house, many of which were built in the 1930s to house the workers. Although houses were built within the park, they proved to be inadequate and Flixton, Urmston and Davyhulme became a desirable place to live for those who worked in the park.

In 1959 more houses were demolished as the motorway, which was opened in 1960, sliced through Urmston and Davyhulme, cutting across two of the area's major roads, Lostock Road and Stretford Road, the latter being particularly affected with such large houses as Urmston Lodge and Auburn Lodge being lost.

Flixton House, 1929. Justice Ralph Wright, the most prominent man in Flixton in the early nineteenth century, built Flixton House in 1806 as an annex to his existing farmhouse. Justice Wright is best known for his closure of a public footpath which ran across his land called the Bottoms Path.

Flixton House, 1936, with the fountain in the foreground after the extension.

Shawe Hall in 1955 before demolition. Shawe Hall was probably built by the Valentine family who were one of the earliest landowners in Flixton and lived in Shaw Town, the area around the Roebuck Hotel, as early as 1305. The hall was originally surrounded by a moat. There is said to have been a tunnel between the Hall and Flixton church. There is some evidence of this to be found in an old surveyor's book in Chethams Library. It talks of the road between Shawtown and the church being widened and a 'causey' found 'under the soil all the length'. The Hall was demolished in 1955.

Davyhulme Hall viewed from the grounds. Davyhulme Hall was the seat of John de Hulme in the reign of Henry II (1154–1189). Robert Norreys lived there in the 1880s, leaving the Hall to his nephew who donated the land on which St Mary's church is built. The estate now belongs to Davyhulme Golf Club.

Davyhulme Hall, showing the entrance gates and driveway.

Urmston Hall, Manor Avenue, 1912. The seat of the ancient families of Urmston was Urmston Hall. Excavations reveal traces of two buildings. The first was half-timbered and can be dated from the late sixteenth to early seventeenth century. The second building was brick and was dated to the 1720s.

Urmston Hall Farm, 1882.

Jawbones Cottage, Davyhulme Road, once one of the entrances to Davyhulme Hall. At one time the entrance had an arch made of pure whalebone. When the Hall was demolished in 1888 the arch was moved to the garden of this cottage on the estate; the cottage still stands.

Newcroft Farm. This farm and Newcroft Hall lay on the land on which Newcroft Road is now situated. The original Hall at Newcroft was surrounded by a moat and dates from the thirteenth century; the lands in the area being given to Richard de Trafford by Adam de Ormston in 1219. The Hall has had a varied history and was owned by such families as the Warburtons and the Hulme family of Davyhulme. Richard Radcliffe lived at Newcroft with his wife Mary in the sixteenth century. He was a famous soldier who was Captain of the Salford muster in the army of his cousin, the Earl of Essex, in 1569. His daughter was one of Queen Elizabeth I's ladies of the bed-chamber. He is buried in Flixton church where there is a brass tablet in his memory. The Hall was finally demolished in 1935 to make way for a new housing estate.

Urmston Hall, around 1900, when the property was being worked as a farm. Mr and Mrs Bancroft are standing in front of the Hall.

The Lindens, Lostock Road, 1890. Situated on the same side as the Nag's Head this photograph shows the children of the Estill family.

Wilderspool House which was situated where the Travel Inn at the Trafford Centre stands today. The Inn was built amongst the trees of Wilderspool Wood.

FLIXTON ROAD. FLIXTON.

(1920) J. GILBODY'S COTTAGE STOOD WHERE TREVOR RD NOW IS.

Gilbodys Cottage, 1920, Trevor Road now stands here. According to an entry in a street directory in 1920, Mrs Gilbody lived alone in this house. The cottage was demolished in 1930.

Ennenda, Church Road, next to
Caius House School, in the 1900s.

Ciss Lane Cottage, 1879. This cottage stood where Higher Road meets Ciss Lane.

Urmston Lodge was situated at the corner of Moss Vale Road and Stretford Road. It was also known as Pineapple Hall as it had three pineapples carved in stone over the front door. It was the residence of Miss Clementina Trafford, sister of Sir Thomas Trafford. She died there in 1834. The lodge was demolished in 1959 to make way for the motorway.

Auburn Lodge on Stretford Road with the slip road to the M62. It was demolished to make way for the motorway.

The Lodge, Urmston Cemetery. This is now a private residence.

The gas lit interior of No. 5 Crofts Bank Road, 1913. Mrs Ellen Cuthbert is one of the ladies seated at the table.

Five

Religion

St Michael's church, Flixton was founded in the twelfth century by Robert de Latham and as such is the oldest church in the area. Urmston was originally part of Flixton parish until the consecration of St Clements in 1868. At this time the population and importance of Urmston was growing and the schoolroom on Stretford road, which had been used for evening services, was no longer considered sufficient. Davyhulme was still a hamlet in the parish of Barton on Irwell. In the 1880s Henry Norreys of Davyhulme Hall gave land on the now Cornhill Road for a school which was used so successfully as a mission that a new parish was created and St Mary's church was built on land donated by J.B. Norreys Entwistle, Henry Norrey's nephew.

The church played a large role in all parts of the community. The schools were originally formed as church schools, and many social activities were to some extent dictated by the church. In 1579 Queen Elizabeth sent down an ecclesiastical commission to look at the violations of the Sabbath. Power was given to churchwardens, amongst others, to stop such activities as bear-baiting, dancing, hunting, and markets on a Sunday.

Methodism has very strong roots in the area. The first church was built on Moorside Road on land donated by John Woods. Davyhulme became a missionary centre and from here Methodism spread to other localities such as Cadishead, Urmston and Walkden. John Wesley, the founder of Methodism in Manchester, visited Davyhulme five times in all and stayed at Mr Hall's house. John Wesley opened the Methodist church on Good Friday 1779; in 1905 a new church was built on Brook Road.

It was reported in 1778, by the Bishop of Chester, that there were only twelve Catholics in the area and no church. Humphrey de Trafford was one of the twelve, but he had his own private chapel in his grounds. A small public church was then built near the Hall in 1791. As the congregation grew a new church was built in 1868 nearby, called All Saints. In 1962 this church was sold to the Conventional Order of Franciscan Friars as church attendance began to decrease. Monsignor Cannon bought a plot of land in Roseneath Road in 1889 upon which a small iron church was built, the present building not being erected until 1914. St Monica's church was opened in 1950 and Our Lady of the Rosary in 1961.

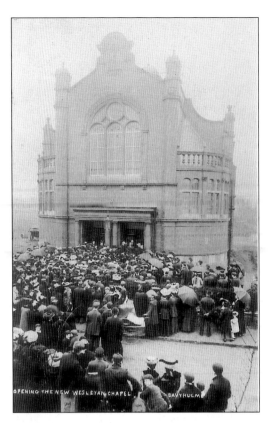

The opening of Brook Road Methodist church, 1905. The new chapel was built because the renovation of the old chapel was found to be too expensive. John Wood, the great-grandson of the donor of the original site, offered the site on Brook Road.

Davyhulme Wesley Methodist Whit Walk, Moorside Road in 1920.

Brook Road Methodist church interior, 1980. The chapel cost in the region of £4,000 to build and was an extremely handsome building with a large organ, choir stalls and beautiful wooden pews. Pews were originally rented and allocated.

Moorside Road Wesleyan chapel. John Wesley came to preach at this church at its opening but he had to speak from a horse block outside the church as there were too many people to fit inside the building. The lighting of this chapel would be by oil lamps and candles. The last service was held here on Easter Sunday 1905.

Methodist Mission which started in Thomas Woodnett's Cottage on Woodsend Road. The mission was a great success and culminated in a new church being opened on Irlam Road in 1894.

Methodist chapel, Irlam Road, Flixton. This chapel was built when the converted cottage used for meetings became too small. Collection began for a new building which was opened in 1894. It was extended in 1927 and 1956.

Methodist church, George Street, Urmston. Methodist meetings were held as early as 1813 in the house of 'Butcher Booth'. 1n 1872 a new church was built in George Street followed by another in 1905, which fronted onto George Street and was opened by the Lord Mayor of Manchester.

The Methodist chapel, seen here in 1939, stood on the north side of Davyhulme Road at the corner with Dalveen Avenue.

Wesley Cottage, the home of James Bent. In the Autumn of 1785, James Bent, a weaver, who lived in Moorside road, gathered the children from the surrounding area in his loom shop on Sunday afternoon for religious instruction. The loom shop was soon not large enough for the numbers and in 1786 the Sunday school was transferred to the chapel were it remained for sixty years.

St Clement's church, 1902, showing the erection of the tower. The site and the grounds of the church were a gift from Col. Ridehalgh. The original building was designed by Mr Medland Taylor of Manchester to accommodate 360 people. It was widened in 1874 and again in 1888; the tower was added in 1902. The clock was a gift from the Reade family to commemorate Thomas James Reade and was dedicated to him in 1906.

St Clement's Sunday School Whit Walks, c. 1900. The procession is on Railway Road, and the houses in the background are on Higher Road.

St Mary's church, Davyhulme Road, c. 1920. The parish of Davyhulme was formed in 1890, and although it was three times the area of Flixton and Urmston, the population was only 1,326 when the church was built. The foundation stone was laid in 1889 and the church was consecrated in 1890. Mrs Isabella Bowers left £2,000 in her Will to help fund the building of the church. In 1959 the Conventional District of Christ Church, Davyhulme, was created as the population of the area grew.

Congregational church, Flixton Road, 1977. This church was opened in 1901 and demolished in 1978 when it was found to be full of dry rot. The congregation joined the Baptists at Greenfield Road and formed the Greenfield church.

Urmston Baptist Church, Greenfield Avenue, 1977. This church was built in 1903 and was without an ordained minister until 1919. In 1975 the Congregationalists joined the church and it became known as Greenfield church.

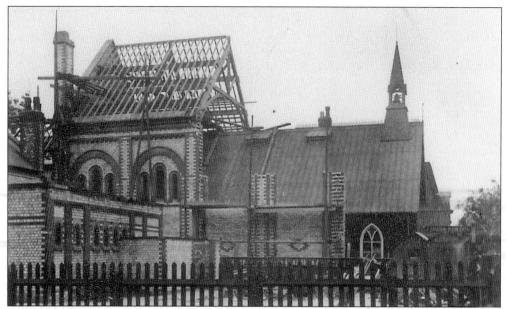

English Martyrs' church, Roseneath Road, 1913. It was built by J. Spark around the old iron church which was then taken down from inside. The foundation stone was laid in 1913.

St Catherine's church, Barton. The parish of St Catherine's, Barton-on-Irwell was formed out of the parish of Eccles in 1867. The land on which the church was built was donated by Sir Thomas de Trafford and the first stone was laid by his wife, Lady de Trafford on 22 July 1842. The church was consecrated on 25 October 1843.

Jewish Chapel and burial ground, Chapel Grove, Urmston, 1976. On the 1896 Ordnance Survey map the burial ground is separated into plots for Polish Jews and Portuguese Jews.

St Michael's church, Flixton, 1910. Although this church is the oldest church in the area, the east wall of the chancel is all that remains of the medieval church. The present church is basically Georgian. The nave and aisles were built in 1756; the tower was rebuilt in 1731 and again in 1889. The earliest stone in the graveyard is dated 1669 although there are records of burials prior to that date. In 1877 the Georgian furnishings were removed and replaced by the stone font, reredos and pulpit. The pulpit was given by the Stott family who owned the mill on Flixton Road.

The Independent chapel, Higher Road, Urmston.

St Clement's church, Whit Walks, 1968.

Six

Education

The first schools in Flixton, Urmston and Davyhulme were church schools, the oldest being St Michael's School which was opened in 1643. The Squire of Flixton, Peter Egerton, gave a cottage next to the Church Inn for use as a school. Most children had to pay to go to the school although there were several free places for poor children. A new school was built in 1662 in front of the Roebuck Hotel. By 1861 a plot of land had been donated by William Worthington Wright, opposite St Michael's church, and this was used to build a larger school. In 1868 the governors of the school applied for a grant but it was not until 1891 that free elementary education was introduced.

St Mary's School was first mentioned in May 1792 and was established with a total donation of £5 5s from various parishioners. The school was built on land bought from John Heywood on Davyhulme Road. All the children had to pay to attend the school. It cost 3d a week for reading and an extra 3d to learn writing, arithmetic and bookkeeping. In 1866 twenty-four out of forty pupils received 3s a quarter from Bradshaws charity to help pay for their fees.

St Clement's School opened in 1859 and stood at Nos 174-180 Stretford Road. These schools soon became inadequate and overcrowded and a second school was built on Higher Road in 1889. In 1972 Lancashire County Education Authority took over the management of the school and in 1974 it came under the control of Trafford Education Department.

Davyhulme Wesley Methodist School opened in 1854, although prior to this date a Sunday School founded in 1846 had taught children to read and write. The school was situated on Moorside Road. Parents had again to pay for their children in the early years. It cost 2d a week for under five year olds, 3d a week for six year olds upwards and 4d a week for the older children.

The Catholic churches also provided schools. St Monica's School opened in 1959; Our Lady of the Rosary being the other primary school. St Paul's Secondary Modern School was then opened in 1961.

As the population grew the need for schools increased and Urmston Higher Grade School opened in 1882. The school was undenominational and received funding from various societies as well as from the Government. The school had a good reputation and in 1886 two pupils won scholarships to Manchester Grammar. However the school served a large area and soon became unable to cope with the number of potential pupils. A larger school was built in Ross Grove and an extension soon followed in Wycliffe Road. In 1923 this school became known as the Grammar School and moved to Newton Road premises in 1929. In 1961 the girls and boys were separated, the boys going to new premises on Bradfield Road. The school is now integrated again, both boys and girls attending the site at Newton Road. The Bradfield Road building has been demolished and houses built on the land.

Flixton Secondary School was opened in 1933. The school was for both girls and boys but as the numbers grew it split into two in 1955, the boys going to a new school on Irlam Road called Wellacre School.

St Michael's School in the 1930s. This was situated on Church Road and remained in use until the 1970s when it was demolished and a new school built.

St Clement's Church School, Stretford Road. In 1858 plans were made to build a school to accommodate the children of Urmston who had previously had to walk to Flixton to acquire their education. A foundation stone was laid by Mr John Hibbert and the school flourished. The building was also used for church services on Sundays conducted by the curate from Flixton.

St Clement's Church School, Higher Road. This school opened on 4 February 1889. It had places for 680 pupils and was later enlarged in 1912. A four-day bazaar helped fund the extension.

St Clement's Church Sunday School, *c.* 1920. The school is gathered on the sports field at the junction of Marshbrook Road and Moorside Road. The houses in the background face onto Roseneath Road.

Two views of St Mary's School, Davyhulme, 1890. In 1880 a new school was built on land given by Squire Norreys of Davyhulme Hall. It was called St Mary's National school and was situated on Cornhill Road or School Lane as it was then called. The school was damaged by fire in 1891 and a new building was built in 1973 at a cost of £45,000.

Two classes at St Mary's School, 1890.

Wesley Methodist School, Moorside Road. The Fold is situated where this school once stood. The children were taught by candle light until 1871 when gas was installed. When this school closed the children went to Flixton County School on Delamere Road which was opened in 1911.

Humphrey Park Branch church, 1949. The interior of this church was used as a day school.

110

Higher Grade School, Urmston, 1920. From left to right, back row: Gwen Morris, Ruth Knowles, Gertrude Kidney, Grace Nichols, Mr Fletcher (head teacher). Centre row: Mr Vaughn, Madge Graham, Hilda Brown, Gertie Wilde, Beatrice Pye, Miss Fletcher (assistant head teacher). Front row: Ronald Boxer, Arthur Black.

Urmston Council Infants School, 1912. This building was originally the extension of Urmston Higher Grade School.

Rose Queen, Urmston Council School, 1921. The children are watching the procession of the Rose Queen in the schoolyard.

Urmston Elementary School's sports day, 1910.

Urmston Council Junior School, 1937.

Wellacre Junior School, 1953, with the official opening by Dame Florence Horsbrough. This school is situated opposite the secondary school on Irlam Road.

Urmston Grammar School, 1973. At this time the school was attended by girls.

The staff of Flixton Girls' School. Miss Wearing, the headmistress, is sitting on the front row, fourth from the left. The hall was originally divided by a partition as it was used by both the boys' school and the girls' school. The quadrangle sides were open to the weather with no corridors.

Seven

Health and Welfare

In 1010, by edict of King Ethelred, one third of the church tithe was to be given to the poor. Traditionally the Church has been heavily involved with the relief of the poor and in 1535 Church Wardens were responsible for keeping alms boxes in the churches. In 1536 the poor were made the legal responsibility of the parish under supervision of the magistrates. In 1597 the first official Poor Rate was levied, taking away some of the responsibilities from the church. In Urmston, Flixton and Davyhulme, various charities were also run. Peter Warburton de Brook left a sum of sixty pounds per annum which helped to educate poor children and rebuild the workhouse. John Wood made provisions for the schooling of poor children in his Will in 1779. In 1786 William Gregory gave ten pounds to supply bread for the poor of Urmston; the money was used to buy a small field which was rented out for two pounds per annum which was paid to a baker who provided the bread. Richard Newton, John Gregory and John Bradshaw of Davyhulme also bequeathed money, mostly for the education of the poor.

Friendly Societies and Sick Clubs were formed. The Flixton Sunday School Company was set up on 12 February 1821 for the relief of the sick, and the Flixton Clothing and Coal Club was established by Mrs Norris of Davyhulme Hall.

Previous to the Poor Law Act of 1834, overseers were appointed who could erect poor houses and levy the poor tax off the householders of the parish. The poor were not allowed to leave the parish without special permission. Poor Houses were set up in Flixton on Moorside Road, and in Urmston on Stretford Road. This building was known as 'The Barracks' and was sold by auction for £200 at the Nelson Hotel in 1857, and was then demolished in 1859. Barton Poor Law Union was formed in 1859 and the old workhouse in Green Lane, Eccles, was reopened. This union catered for the Flixton, Urmston and Davyhulme areas. The Flixton and Urmston elected guardians were Thomas Leach and William Warbrook. The union cared for the sick, poor and the old, as well as providing work for the able bodied.

In 1924 it was reported in the minute book of the Barton Upon Irwell Guardians that an application for the purchase of land for a hospital in Davyhulme was made, and in December 1928 the first patients were transferred from the Green Lane Institute. Only the ones expected to survive were transferred. The hospital continued to expand and serve the community until it was taken over by the War Office during the Second World War to be used by the armed forces.

In 1894 Davyhulme sewage works were built to serve an escalating population. They were the biggest in the North West. Four ships were used to carry the sludge down the Manchester Ship Canal to the Irish Sea.

Laying of the foundation stone of Park Hospital by the Earl of Derby and Sir Thomas Robinson on 2 July 1926. The first managers of Park Hospital were the Guardians of Barton-Upon-Irwell Union.

Park Hospital, 1929. The official opening of the hospital was June 1929. It was opened by HRH Princess Mary Viscountess Lascelles. By this time the management of the hospital had transferred to the Lancashire County Council in accordance with the 1929 Local Government Act.

Park Hospital, 1929. This is the board room in the hospital.

The entrance hall to Park Hospital, 1929.

Park Hospital, 1929. A ward showing the veranda that was built on the end of every ward to provide light and fresh air to the patients.

The staff at Park Hospital welcome Mr Bevan, 1948. Aneurin Bevan, the Minister of Health, introduced the National Health Service Act in 1946. The purpose of the Act was to take over all hospitals on 5 July 1948.

Aneurin Bevan meets officials, 5 July 1948. Mr Bevan visited Park Hospital on the first day of the National Heath Service. The keys of Park Hospital were handed over to him at a ceremony at the hospital on this day. This was a great honour for the hospital, one which was conferred on only two other hospitals in the whole of the country. He said in his speech, 'This is a wonderful hospital you are running. It is in excellent condition and we are taking it over as a going concern.'

Cottage Hospital, Greenfield Avenue, 1976. In 1897, the year of Queen Victoria's jubilee, the local people wanted to erect a permanent memorial. The scheme for the hospital was hit upon and fund raising started. The hospital opened in 1900 and provided care for those unable to afford care in their own homes. The hospital eventually became a maternity hospital and is now a nursing home.

Dr Maine on horseback outside a house in Lily Street (now Grosvenor Road), 1900. The local people depended on local doctors for their health needs. However this was not a free service for most until the National Health Service was implemented in 1948.

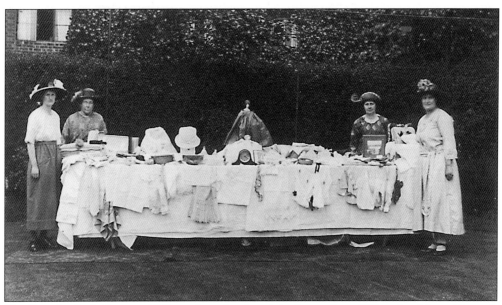

The Cripples Help Society, 1920, with a sale of work in the garden of Waverley, Moorside road. The owner was Mrs Crossfield (far right) with Mrs Shackleton next to her. The cottages in the background are on the other side of the road next to the White House, although they have now been demolished.

Eight

Wartime

Urmston, Flixton and Davyhulme, like everywhere else, was affected by the two world wars. Many families suffered loss and a roll of the dead can be seen on the war memorial on the Nags Head Circle, and the memorial in Urmston on Crofts Bank Road near Golden Hill Park.

Two Red Cross hospitals were opened for the treatment and convalescence of soldiers and refugees. Wibbersley, a private residence in beautiful grounds, was offered by Dr and Mrs Smith of Altrincham. The hospital could accommodate 101 patients but this was soon proved to be inadequate and another building called Oakfield was offered by Miss Hand. This later became a residence for the nurses. Flixton Institute was then offered by the committee and was used as an extension to Wibbersley. Much of the equipment for the hospital was loaned by local residents.

Trafford Park lay very close to Davyhulme and paid an important role in the Second World War. Factories such as Metrovicks were asked to produce bombers. Two machine guns were placed on the top of the Liverpool warehousing buildings, two barrage balloon stations were set up and Trafford Hall was taken over by the military. This affected the local area as with the men going to war, many women went to work in Trafford Park and found themselves succeeding in jobs they would never have previously considered. Trafford Park and the Manchester Ship Canal were heavily bombed leading to more bombs being dropped on an area that otherwise would not have been targeted. Both the Urmston and Stretford authorities dug air-raid shelters all over Trafford Park to protect the workers. Two destroyers were adopted by the civil community of Urmston, HMS *Express* and HMS *Zebra*.

The locals also had their share of prisoners of war. On the ground which is now Kingsway Park, near Lostock Road, there was a camp which housed four anti-aircraft guns. There were wooden huts for housing the gun crews, canteens and store facilities. The guns were removed in 1940 and the camp used for prisoners of war, firstly Italians and later Germans. The prisoners used to work on the locals farms and were allowed out on their own to get fresh milk from Croft Farm.

In 1939 Park Hospital was requisitioned by the War Office to be used as a military hospital first for the British army then for the American army. Many residents were asked to house American soldiers.

Wibbersley House hospital, 29 October 1914. This photograph shows Belgian soldiers outside the hospital; they were the first of the wounded to be sent to Wibbersley. As well as numerous

entertainments put on by such groups as the Local Operatic Society, there was a visit by the Belgian State Operatic Artists.

The war memorial at the Nag's Head roundabout, 1920, with Bethels Farm in the background. The memorial now holds names of the dead from both the First and Second World Wars.

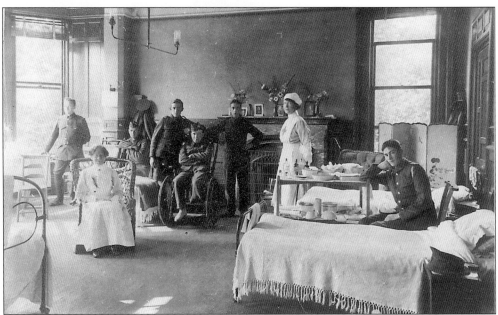

Ward One at Wibbersley, 1915, which shows patients and staff in a converted bedroom. By August 1915, 342 patients had been admitted comprising of 229 British, 87 Belgians, 20 Australians, 5 Canadians and 1 New Zealander. There were ample facilities for outdoor recreation and visits were made to the two picture houses in Urmston.

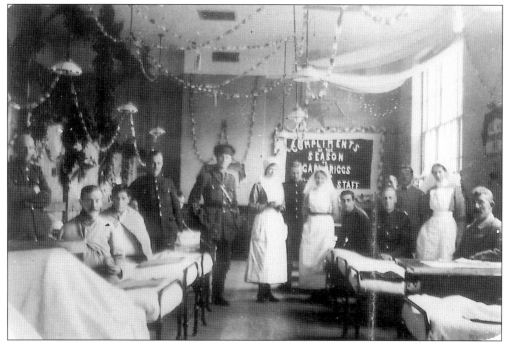

Christmas at Wibbersley Hospital during the First World War.

Wibbersley Hospital No. 2, 1918. Flixton Institute building at the corner of Flixton Road and Delamere Road. This hospital accommodated forty beds arranged in three wards as well as a dining room and staff room.

The Victory Parade on Crofts Bank Road, 19 July 1919. All over the country Victory celebrations were in progress In Urmston various treats were organized for the day. Tea was provided in the drill hall in Flixton Road for all residents who had reached the age of sixty.

The Victory Parade crossing Urmston Bridge, 1919. All children who had applied for an Invitation Card to join the procession around the parish received a free tea after the parade. Sporting events were held on Acre Gate field on Flixton Road and included potato races and skipping races. In the evening Mr J. Augustus Riley's Concert Party provided a series of outdoor concerts and the Higher Broughton Brass band were in attendance.

The Victory Parade on Station Road Urmston, 1919. After a Thanksgiving Service the parade set off down Flixton Road, Brook Road, Moorside Road, Woodsend Road, Irlam Road, Flixton Road, round the Jubilee Tree and along Flixton to the field.

The Victory Parade at the junction of Stretford Road, Queens Road and Church Road 1919. The public were invited to decorate the route of the procession and the children encouraged to carry flags.

Land Girls working on Urmston Meadows, 1940. Although many women worked in Trafford Park, many women chose to work on the land as part of the war effort. Any spare land was used to grow food and crops.

Land Girls in Urmston Cemetery. The girls in the land army are shown here growing crops in the cemetery.